COMPILED BY JULIE FAIRHURST

WOMEN LIKE ME

Community

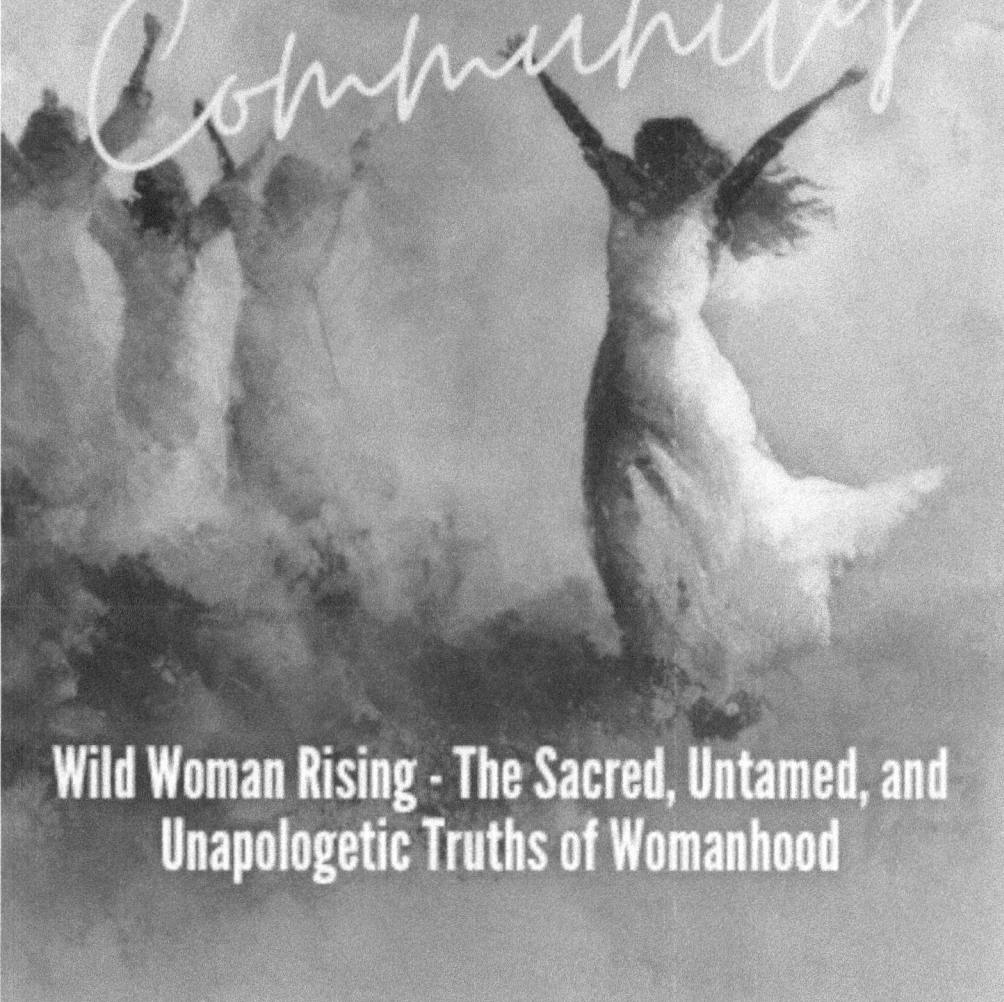

Wild Woman Rising - The Sacred, Untamed, and Unapologetic Truths of Womanhood

Compiled by Julie Fairhurst
Paperback Edition: ISBN:978-1-990639-33-3
Interior & Cover Design by STOKE Publishing
Manuscript Editing by Tammie Trites

Publisher:
Rock Star Publishing British Columbia, Canada
Email: julie@changeyourpath.ca

WOMEN LIKE ME COMMUNITY

WILD WOMAN RISING: THE SACRED, UNTAMED, UNAPOLOGETIC TRUTHS OF WOMANHOOD

JULIE FAIRHURST

ROCK STAR PUBLISHING

CONTENTS

*I dedicate Wild Woman Rising to all the amazing, outstanding,
caring, beautiful, and brave women of
Write Like a Woman – Empowered by Women Like Me.*

*You are the heart of this movement,
the storytellers, the truth-tellers, the healers, and the dreamers.*

*With every word you write, you rise, and with every rise,
you lift another woman higher.*

*This book is for you.
For your fire, your softness, your courage, and your voice.*

"Elegance is a glowing inner peace. Grace is an ability to give as well as to receive and be thankful. Mystery is a hidden laugh always ready to surface! Glamour only radiates if there is a sublime courage & bravery within: glamour is like the moon; it only shines because the sun is there."
C. JoyBell C.

COLLABORATIVE PUBLICATION

This is a collaborative publication, and you may notice variations in writing style from one piece to another. This is intentional, as it allows each writer to share their story in its authentic voice, preserving the uniqueness of their contribution.

We believe their raw and genuine perspectives bring a richness to this collection that polished writing alone cannot capture.

Each story reflects the individual journey and truth of the writer, which we honor and celebrate.

Some of these women are "first-time authors, not professional writers, but they have poured their hearts and experiences into these pages.

Every woman participating in the Women Like Me program shares a common purpose: "If my story can help even one person, then sharing it is truly worthwhile.

"Don't think about making women fit the world --
think about making the world fit women."
~Gloria Steinem~

DISCLOSURE

Dear Beautiful Reader,

Before you dive into the powerful, soul-stirring stories that make up the Women Like Me book series, I want to offer you a gentle heads-up, heart-to-heart.

These pages are rich with truth, courage, and the kind of resilience that rises from the ashes of real-life struggle. But as inspiring as these stories are, they're not a replacement for professional medical, psychological, or therapeutic support. These aren't prescriptions, they're lived experiences, raw, honest, and beautifully human.

And sometimes? They hit deep.

If you find yourself feeling overwhelmed or triggered as you read, please don't carry it alone. Reach out. Talk to someone you trust, a friend, a counselor, a therapist. Let someone hold space for you while you process. Asking for support is not weakness, it's wisdom, it's strength, and it's one of the bravest things you'll ever do.

This journey isn't about doing it all on your own. It's about walking together, with grace, grit, and the full-hearted knowing that healing is possible.

So go ahead, flip these pages. Let the words meet you where you are. Let the voices of these incredible women remind you that your story matters, your voice is valid, and your strength is already within you, just waiting to be remembered.

Now, let's begin, side by side, with courage, compassion, and a whole lot of heart.

With love and belief in you,

Julie Fairhurst

Founder, Women Like Me

"Kindness is universal. Sometimes being kind allows others to see the goodness in humanity through you.
Always be kinder than necessary."
~Germany Kent~

THE WILD WOMAN'S PRAYER

May we speak when silenced,
Love when hardened,
Soften when shamed,
Rise when told to sit down.

May our laughter echo through generations,
And our truth burn through the lies,
We are not broken, we are blooming,
We are not lost, we are becoming,

We are not too much,
We are exactly enough,
And we are rising.

By Julie Fairhurst

*This poem was written after compiling this book
and reading the incredible stories shared within its pages.*

"Each time a woman stands up for herself,
she stands up for all women."
∼Maya Angelou∼

INTRODUCTION

There's a wildness that lives in every woman, sometimes whispering, sometimes roaring, that refuses to be silenced. It is not chaos. It is not rebellion for its own sake. It is the call of truth that beats beneath centuries of conditioning, urging us to remember who we were before the world told us who to be.

It is not recklessness; it is remembrance. A call from somewhere ancient that says, "You were never meant to shrink."

The Wild Woman is not one face, one story, or one lifetime. She is a chorus of archetypes rising through us, shaping how we love, create, fight, and rise again.

She is the **Maiden**, untamed curiosity and wide-eyed wonder, daring to dance barefoot into possibility.

She is the **Mother**, the nurturer and creator, birthing life, art, and revolutions from the chaos of her own becoming.

She is the **Warrior**, scarred yet unbroken, protecting her truth with both tenderness and fire.

She is the **Wise Woman**, steady and seasoned, carrying the medicine of experience and the quiet knowing that only time can teach.

She is the **Mystic**, guided by intuition, sensing the unseen threads that connect us all.

And she is the **Alchemist**, turning heartbreak into wisdom, pain into purpose, and loss into legacy.

Together, these women live within us, sometimes clashing, sometimes harmonizing, reminding us that we are allowed to be both sacred and scarred, both soft and steel.

To be a wild woman is to live unapologetically, to feel everything deeply, and to speak the truths we were once told to bury. It's the art of rising again and again, not because the world gave us permission, but because our souls demanded it.

This book is a gathering of those voices. Women who dare to rise.

Women who have shed their masks, walked through their fires, and emerged radiant in their truth. These are the sacred, tamed, and unapologetic stories of womanhood. Fierce, vulnerable, beautiful, and breathtakingly honest.

Each woman in these pages did something wild and holy; she let herself be seen. She peeled back the layers of "fine" and "I'm okay" and stood, heart open, in the whole light of her truth.

That's no small thing. That's the revolution.

These authors dared to write their stories and their poetry, raw, tender, unfiltered. And in doing so, they turned toward the sun. They said, "Here I am. This is what it means to be a woman, sacred, scarred, tamed, and untamed all at once."

Their words shimmer with bravery. Their honesty is a mirror, showing us the parts of ourselves we've kept in shadow. And as the sun shines on them, we see them, not as victims of their stories, but as creators of new ones.

This is what it means to rise: to stand in your truth, to let your wild heart be witnessed, and to remind the world that light was never meant to hide.

Here they are, our Wild Women Rising.

To every woman who reads this: you are not too much, too loud, or too wild. You are exactly as you were meant to be... a living embodiment of every woman who came before you.

Welcome to the rising.

Julie Fairhurst

Founder of Women Like Me

"The question that women casually shopping for perfume ask more than any other is this: "What scent drives men wild?" After years of intense research, we know the definitive answer. It is bacon. Now, on to the far more interesting subject of perfume."
~Tania Sanchez~

PART 1

WILD WOMAN RISING

THE SACRED, UNTAMED, UNAPOLOGETIC TRUTHS OF WOMANHOOD

A DECADE IN THE FIRE – MY MENOPAUSE JOURNEY

THERESA WAUGH

For ten years, I've walked through the slow-burning fire of menopause, facing sleepless nights, tidal waves of emotion, and a battle to reclaim myself. This is my story of struggle, awakening, and the powerful decision to live for me.

It's been ten years since my body quietly began closing a chapter I never realized would be so brutal to endure. I had heard about menopause in hushed conversations, in the back corners of coffee shops, or in half-hearted jokes about "hot flashes" and "getting old." What no one told me, what no one prepared me for, was the storm that would rage inside me for a decade, threatening to take away not just my comfort, but pieces of my identity.

At first, it was small, almost imperceptible. A skipped period. An odd night where sleep just... didn't come. Then, the heat started waves of fire that rolled through my chest and neck like molten lava, leaving me drenched in sweat in the middle of meetings or awake at three a.m. in soaked pajamas. My skin prickled with heat, and I'd throw off the blankets only to pull them back moments later when chills set in.

My body was no longer mine, it was an unpredictable machine, flipping switches I couldn't control.

But the physical symptoms were only the surface. The deeper cuts came from the emotional side effects. I had always prided myself on being steady, patient, and composed. Suddenly, I was living with an anger I didn't recognize. A spark of irritation could become a wildfire in seconds. The sound of someone chewing too loudly. A driver cutting me off. A comment I might have brushed off in the past now lodged itself in my chest like a splinter, and the anger would burn hot and fast.

And then, the sadness.

It wasn't the kind of sadness that made me cry for a day and then move on, it was the heavy, creeping kind that seeped into my mornings and followed me to bed. It made me feel invisible, even in rooms full of people who loved me. My children, now older, didn't need me the same way they once had. Some days, the tears weren't about anything tangible. Sometimes, I just felt hollow.

Over the years, the symptoms came in waves, insomnia, brain fog so thick I'd forget why I walked into a room, weight gain that clung stubbornly despite my best efforts, and a fatigue that made even simple errands feel like a marathon.

I began to feel disconnected from myself, as though I was watching my life happen from the outside. I'd put on the smile, show up to events, and make sure everyone else was comfortable, but inside, I was running on empty.

It took me a long time to realize I had fallen into a trap. For years, decades even, I had been the caretaker, the peacemaker, the one who smoothed rough edges and made sure everyone else's needs were met. I had learned to put myself second, third, or last if that's what it took to keep the people around me happy. I told myself it was love that it was strength. And maybe sometimes it was. But menopause stripped away my ability to keep up the act without cost.

The truth was, "I wasn't just tired" from night sweats and insomnia, I was tired of myself. Tired of swallowing my words. Tired of pretending I wasn't upset when I was. Tired of bending so far to accommodate everyone else that I couldn't remember the shape of my own life.

One day, in the middle of yet another moment of emotional exhaustion, I stopped. I saw my reflection in the window, flushed, tear-streaked, exhausted, and I realized: This isn't about them. This is about me. Somewhere along the line, I had become so focused on being "good" for everyone else that I had abandoned being good to myself.

It was a strange gift, that moment of clarity.

Menopause had taken so much from me, it had shaken my confidence, tested my resilience, and challenged my sanity. But in the process, it had also stripped me bare. With nothing left to hide behind, I finally had to face the truth: I had been living to please everyone else, and in doing so, I had forgotten how to please myself.

Now, I don't care what people think of me. I don't care if they judge me. I am not living my life to meet their expectations or fit into their definition of "acceptable." I am living my life for me, for what brings me joy, for what makes my heart light, for what allows me to wake up each morning feeling free instead of burdened.

Since then, I've started small. I say "no" when I need to, without guilt. I rest when my body demands it, even if the laundry isn't folded. I speak my mind more often, even when my voice shakes.

I've picked up hobbies just for me, things that don't serve a purpose except to make me smile. I've learned to let go of the pressure to be everything for everyone, because the truth is, I can't be, and I don't need to be.

Menopause is still here with me. Some nights, the heat still wakes me. Some days, my emotions still pull me under without warning. But now, I see these moments differently. They are not just symptoms, they are signals. They remind me to slow down, to check in with myself, to make sure I'm not losing me again in the shuffle of taking care of everyone else.

I wish I could go back to my younger self and tell her: "You don't need permission to live for yourself". I wish I could tell her that "being kind and loving doesn't mean sacrificing your joy, your rest, or your dreams". That saying "I matter" isn't selfish, it's survival.

Now, when I feel that flicker of anger or that heaviness of sadness, I try to meet it with compassion. I ask myself what I need, instead of what I can give. And I've learned something I wish every woman could know: You are allowed to choose you, unapologetically.

Ten years of menopause have taught me many things, but the most important lesson is this, life is too short to spend it molding yourself into what others need while neglecting the person you truly are.

The truth is the people who love you will love you more when you are whole. And the ones who don't? Let them go.

So, here's what I know now, deep in my bones:

Live your life for you. Not for the expectations, not for the approval, not for the comfort of others.

Live it for the things that make you wake up with excitement, for the moments that make you laugh so hard your cheeks hurt, for the quiet nights where you feel peace just being in your own company.

Because at the end of the day, your happiness is not a luxury, it's a gift from the creator and we need to live it to the fullest.

"May the love in your heart overshadow any sorrows, and may you always know with a deep inner certainty, how loved you truly are."
~Jodi Livon~

MY WILD SOUL
THERESA CAMPBELL

I have always known that I have a wild soul. I am sacred. I am wisdom. I am light. My knowing comes from an ancient place, perhaps the wisdom of my ancestors who lived on this land, suffered, thrived and died here. I could never explain it. Even as a child of three or four years old, I just knew I was connected to something powerful.

My ancestors were farmers. They arrived in Canada in the 1840's, originally from Scotland, Ireland and Sweden. I believe their experiences have shaped my psyche.

As a small child, I felt compelled to dance in the fields around our farmhouse. My tiny body was filled with an inspiration I could not explain. The dance was a form of celebration and praise. Happy to be alive, I danced with wonder and gratitude. The trees, the birds and the flowers were my inspiration.

Because of the size of our family, and four siblings below me requiring my mother's divided attention, I was sent to school one year ahead of my peers. Kindergarten was not available in the mid 1960's so I was enrolled in grade one at the age of five.

I met this challenge with courage and optimism. I remember tripping on the steps boarding the large yellow school bus. The driver patiently smiled, "Are you alright?"

"Yes," I managed to respond, swallowing my pain and embarrassment. I considered it was not acceptable to cry. This was my first day of school. I was liberated from a turbulent household filled with crying babies and restless toddlers; one brother having been diagnosed with autism. I simply had to be strong now.

I arrived at school and felt incredibly welcomed. The teacher had decorated the classroom door with art, a beautiful tree surrounded by little red apples with a student name on each one. I found my name and immediately felt I belonged here. This was my community, even if my peers were older, taller, possibly possessed more social skills than I. It didn't matter. I could learn here, whatever I was supposed to learn, as long as I could hold onto my "wild soul."

It was September and the routine began, waking early, eating breakfast, grabbing my lunch bag and boarding the bus at the end of our lane way, five days a week. I had to follow a schedule, sit quietly, listen and do my work.

I attended Catholic School. We said prayers, stood for God Save the Queen and O Canada every morning. I learned pride of place and humility. I also learned the consequences of stepping out of line.

One day, I was sitting at my desk in the classroom along with my peers, focused on my work when suddenly, the atmosphere in the room changed. Our teacher had momentarily stepped into the hallway and closed the door.

Some students became excited and spontaneously decided to get up and form a circle around the perimeter of the room. For no apparent reason, I joined them.

We held hands and danced in a circle around the perimeter of the room. Engaged in this communal dance, my body unintentionally grazed a flowerpot which sat precariously on the edge of our teacher's desk. It hit the floor and at that moment, our teacher entered the room.

All eyes and fingers were pointed at me. I froze in horror as my peers retreated to their desks with lightning speed. I felt abandoned. My face was ashen with shame. How did this happen? I concluded that my peers could not be trusted. I was alone.

The teacher called me into a private space and questioned me about the incident. My emotions were high, but I held it together, crying and releasing my shame. On the other hand, I was able to express how unfair it was that almost everyone was dancing around the room, but I was the only one blamed for it. "Yes, I bumped the flowerpot by accident. It wasn't my idea to dance around the room. I just followed. I'm sorry."

I thought I saw Sister Cora smile, but she quickly handed me a tissue saying, "Thank you, you may return to your seat."

We were briefly lectured on the importance of safety and the need for trust, trusting others. I was too overwrought to really hear what our teacher was saying. I felt wounded. That was my initiation, so to speak.

From that moment, I knew I had to trust myself more than my peers. My wild soul knew that people, particularly your peers are prone to whims and strange behaviour that can lead to trouble. I wasn't vying for sainthood. No, I just needed to be authentic and real in a world that continually tries to lead you astray.

As I grew older, in middle grades, I began extra curricular activities. I was a girl guide for a while, then I began figure skating. This sport included skills and artistic choreography, a kind of dance and interpretation of music. It was the artistry that I enjoyed the most. I loved skating to dramatic music, fast and slow. A skating program tells a story and just like an actor, you must feel your story for it to be believable. I believe that my wild soul was happiest when I skated interpretive programs. My soul was free to express itself without apologies.

When I graduated from high school and moved on to university, I knew that my wild soul needed more nurturing, so I studied Humanities, eventually graduating with a degree in English Literature. I always knew stories were my destiny. I just hoped I would hold onto the wild soul, my intuitive side, and not get caught up in peer pressure and politics of pleasing others. As women, we are often expected to please others and often that comes at a cost to our authentic self.

I soon took a job as a reporter for a community newspaper. I reported on local news and personal interest stories. I excelled at the personal interest stories because I found people interesting. I was less successful reporting political stories because I found my need to please was interfering with objectivity. The pressure to please discouraged me from continuing my job as a reporter. I got married and moved to the big city.

I took a new job as an office administrator but soon left that and began a new vocation.

I worked with special needs children. Truth is, I liked being in elementary classrooms and listening to teachers read stories aloud and watching children act out and remembering my experience of acting out and the consequences. It felt real. And yes, I identify with the children who may be unique, perhaps struggling. It reminds me, we all have a wild soul.

"Children move stones with their feet. Men move rocks with their
hands. Women move mountains with their hearts."
~Matshona Dhliwayo~

NEWFOUND CONFIDENCE
JOANNE SMITH

My spouse and I left to spend three of the winter months in Yuma, Arizona, with our RV. We stopped at all our favourite places along the way. Louisiana is our favourite place because of the food and the southern hospitality. Crawfish, boudin, cracklins and bread pudding were always on the menu.

We were also excited to see our friends from the ranch in Alberta. They had a winter home in the same RV park we were headed to. Once we got settled in Yuma, I continued my therapy sessions with Shelly, my therapist, via video.

My spouse assumed I was going to forgo my sessions with Shelly for the three months we were away, and he thought I was fine and didn't need them, anyway. Considering it was his infidelity that set these therapy sessions in motion, I think he may have been feeling a little guilty and ashamed. I am certain these sessions I was having with Shelly reminded him of his indiscretions.

One evening, after my spouse had had a few beers, he started making derogatory comments about my therapy sessions.

Recently, I had been speaking my mind, which he didn't like, so I was quite surprised he entered such uneasy territory. He made several statements about how I needed to get over it, stating that therapy was a crutch and a waste of money. I made no acknowledgement of his comments.

He was unable to bait me into an argument or change my mind. I wish I had been able to see, then, how unsupportive and sabotaging he had been. I did make a mental note, however, not to continue to allow him to influence my decisions for self-care.

A few weeks later, while visiting friends in San Diego, we took a four-day trip up the west coast of California and stopped at a few beaches. We love to walk on the beach. Feeling the warm sand between our toes, watching pelicans dive-bomb into the water to hunt for their prey, hearing the waves crash against the shore and tasting the moist, salty mist on our upper lip never gets old.

We stopped at Laguna Beach, Huntington Beach, and Ocean Beach. About halfway through our trip, my spouse suggested we meet a young lady for lunch in Venice Beach. We had met her on a train trip out to British Columbia four years earlier with my Mama.

Amanda and her sister shared the room next to ours on the train. They were in their early 20s. My spouse made a habit of taking young girls under his wing when we travelled and then keeping in touch with them afterwards through Facebook or Messenger.

We once met two young girls in Montreal while spending a long weekend touring this beautiful historic city on our bikes. He has also kept in touch with these girls. When we travelled to Portugal for three weeks to visit our niece in 2019, my spouse befriended two young girls from Denmark. He had them tour with us and eat with us on several occasions during our stay in Lisbon. I tried to protest, but he told me I was being rude and unsociable.

I must say, there was never a time when I recall meeting two young men on our travels and insisting, they tour with us, nor would I have continued to keep in touch with them.

I was not okay with him doing it either. He made me doubt myself by gaslighting me to believe that it was my behaviour that was inappropriate, not his. After all, we were travelling to meet new people and socialize.

He always asked these young women to join us while I was standing with them. This benefited my spouse in two ways. The young women felt safe going places with him because I was with them, and they did not feel threatened. Secondly, he knew I would not object in front of them, as it would come across as rude or create a scene. So, when he suggested we meet Amanda in Venice Beach, I said "no". I had not kept in touch with her or her sister and did not consider her a friend.

I told Gary it was inappropriate to have kept in contact with all these young girls, and I would no longer support this behaviour. He was very upset with me. He tried to convince me it would be rude because he had already contacted her and said we were coming. I told him I wasn't going and that he would have to cancel or go himself. I tried to explain that when he tries to insert these young women into our lives, it triggers how I felt when he was cheating.

Feelings of not being enough, being rejected for a younger model, and that he will never truly understand how his infidelity has affected me. I asked him to leave the hotel we were staying in for a few hours and let me be alone so I could sort out how I was feeling about it.

While he was gone, I wrote a poem called 'Newfound Confidence.'

Newfound Confidence

Heavy with indignation, I took a stand today,
I refused to be unseen and then controlled,
I demanded to be valued and heard,
No longer duty-bound to fit his mould.

I let him know his behaviour was inappropriate,
I explained why I wasn't going to comply,
When I was finished, he took the coward's way,
He couldn't look at me and didn't reply.

It was then that I realized my power,
My non-acceptance of his attempted deflection,
His demands and attempts to manipulate,
We're met with sureness and a clear perception.

I stood in my newfound confidence,
Not allowing his supremacy to take hold,
Unlike all the times before now,
I allowed my fortitude to freely unfold.

(Feb 13, 2023)

When my spouse returned to the hotel a few hours later, I was confident of two things: one, I would no longer accept unacceptable behaviour from him, and two, I strongly believed he would never understand that this kind of behaviour was inappropriate. If he were reading this right now, he still would not get it.

After realizing this, I decided I couldn't live like this anymore. As the American journalist, commentator and columnist Charles M. Blow once said:

"One doesn't have to operate with great malice to do great harm. The absence of empathy and understanding is sufficient."

A week after we returned to our RV in Yuma, I asked my spouse a question. "If anything, ever happened to us and we split up, would I be able to stay in our home?" Although this thought crossed my mind several times in the last six months to a year, I was afraid to ask.

My worst fear was that I'd give up everything we had built together and everything that made me feel secure. He looked at me and said, "No, you wouldn't have to move out. You didn't do anything wrong, so why would you have to go through the trauma of having to relocate?"

I waited a few days for this conversation to sink in, and then I approached him and said,

"I want a divorce." It was almost like he was expecting it.

He looked slightly surprised but sat silently and waited for me to continue. I said, "I do not believe that you will ever understand the extent to which the trauma of your cheating has affected me. I feel that staying with you will continue to leave me open to being exposed to situations that trigger me. I know that the things you do or say are not meant to upset me intentionally."

"I am sorry, but I can never forgive you for cheating, and I don't expect you to continue to live in this shadow of shame."

He said, "I knew you could never forgive me, and you are right; I don't want to live like this either. We must sort out how we will deal with the business and the house."

Two days later, I had a separation agreement drafted. We both signed it, and our friend from Alberta signed and witnessed it. It is not exactly a legal document, but we both respect each other enough to abide by it.

What a relief!

A week later, we started our journey back home to Canada. It was not without sadness and raw emotion. It was difficult for both of us as we struggled with the upcoming changes that were to transpire.

We had such a busy and wonderful life together before his indiscretions. The lies associated with infidelity cut the deepest. They take from us that we didn't know we were giving up.... our dignity!

We have since worked out the details of our home and our home-based business. I have remained in the house. He has been exceptionally generous financially and comes to the house once a week to do any small repairs or needed yard scaping. We have remained friendly and in touch with our extended families.

Having found the confidence to stand up for myself, I am now in control of my own destiny, and I know my worth.

"She is of the strangest beauty and the darkest courage, and when she walks with intent the earth trembles beneath her feet."
~Nicole Lyons~

CHANGING THE GENERATIONS OF ABUSE
HEATHER CULLEN

Changing the generations of abuse in your family is a hard and difficult road to take. My mother was a victim of abuse as a child by my grandfather. She in turned married a man (my father) that tried to kill her. I in turn married a man who tried to put my head through a car windshield.

Breaking that chain was painful it involved changing the tapes in my head that lead me to find these types of men.

My mom helped break that chain by instilling a sense of courage in me. She was a single mom in the 70's raising two teenage daughters alone after my dad went to jail. that took a great deal of courage.

When she dated if a man raised his voice, she left him.

She finally met my stepfather years later. It was that example of change in her that lead me to recognize my owns partners behaviour and realize when I left my husband with a diaper bag and sixteen-month-old boy I needed help to change the tapes as they call it.

For three years I belonged to a women's group and sought out counselling to change my views, attitudes and learned to love myself first and always. I met my second husband and was blessed with three more boys and lots of love and kindness until he died.

Change and growth is hard and not for the faint hearted but it can be done.

Sometimes its two steps forward and three steps back but building a solid foundation with women around you can help you get there. Gathering the courage to help you get there can make a difference and remembering you are not alone that others have been through this helps.

I now have four grown men that treat their partners in loving caring ways and have healthy relationships built on love, kindness and mutual respect.

The chain can be broken you just have to have the courage to take the first steps.

It's always about timing. If it's too soon, no one understands.
If it's too late, everyone's forgotten."
~Ann Wintour~

Her Name is After

She breaks the chains they forged to bind,
No cage can hold her restless mind,
Her cry splits open the quiet air,
A wild truth, raw beyond repair.

Her scars are banners, her rage a flame,
She will not bend to guilt or shame,
The bones of silence crack beneath,
Her voice, a storm, her breath unsheathed.

She walks through fire, her feet unscarred,
Her stride unyielding, her spirit unmarred,
She claims the dark; she owns the light,
A force unbound, a will of might.

Her eyes are daggers, sharp and clear,
Her laugh defies both cage and fear,
The sacred pulse of blood and skin,
A battle cry that shakes within.

Unapologetic fierceness in her power,
She rises unbroken; she will not cower,
Her truth resounds, defiance her master,
Her name is Strength. Her Name is After.

-Brenda Cooper

"Don't think about making women fit the world -- think about making the world fit women."
~Gloria Steinem~

OUR STORY: A JOURNEY OF LOVE, LOSS, AND RESILIENCE

BRENDA-LEE HUNTER

This story is not so much my story as it is my daughter's. It's a story of beginnings marked by struggle, of a bond forged not by blood but by choice, and of love stretched to its very limits.

Twenty years ago, I stood in the hallway of BC Women's Hospital, outside the Fir Square Unit, a place unlike any other. This unit was reserved for mothers who were giving birth under circumstances that were already steeped in trauma. Addiction, loss, and adversity had touched every life in that ward long before the first cries of any child echoed through it.

I remember the air in the corridor that day. It felt heavy, but also electric. Moments earlier, I had seen a young woman in active labor. Her wrists were bound in shackles, her steps guided by an armed guard. She was escorted to a birthing room like a prisoner, even as her body labored to bring forth new life.

The scene was surreal, its own brand of heartbreak and hope intertwined.

Then came the sound. My daughter's first cries. The sound was both a miracle and a weight. It was life announcing itself despite the odds.

Only moments later, I was ushered into the room, invited to meet the tiny human who would forever change my life. I was asked to cut her umbilical cord, a symbolic act, but one that felt monumental. And just like that, our story together began.

For me, it became a story of opening my heart to a child who had not grown under my heart but rather, inside it. It was a story of learning that love, as powerful as it is, cannot single-handedly heal trauma or rewire a nervous system shaped by adversity.

It was about being her fierce advocate, navigating systems that were not built to understand her needs, and confronting the painful realization that no matter how much I gave, I would often feel I was never quite enough.

For her, it was a story of beginning life at a disadvantage. She was born with addiction in her veins and trauma woven into her earliest experiences. She had no choices in any of it, no say in the loss of her biological mother, no control over the substances that flowed through her blood before she took her first breath. As much as she loved me and relied on me, the pain and anger she carried often landed on the one person who stayed by her side through everything.

And yet, she was a radiant baby. Her laugh was the kind that erupted from her belly and caught everyone in its orbit.

As a toddler, she had a spark in her eyes, mischievous, joyful, and alive. Those early years held so many moments of pure delight. But as she grew from toddler to preschooler and then into grade school, her challenges became impossible to ignore.

By grade three, she was struggling to read anywhere near her grade level. That became my call to arms. I began seeking answers, refusing to let her slip through the cracks of an education system that wasn't built for her brain. When we found the right people, those who understood how her mind worked, she began to thrive.

Those small victories became our lifeline.

Still, new challenges emerged as she grew. By middle school, she was still prone to tantrums that resembled those of a much younger child. I immersed myself in learning how to support a child with impaired executive functioning, taking her to private therapy and specialized tutoring. We muddled through, both of us exhausted but determined.

Then came adolescence. By the time she turned twelve, the mood swings were unrelenting. Self-harm surfaced. She smoked weed for the first time. She became sexually active far too early, ran away from home, experimented with drugs like Molly, and at times became physically abusive. I could feel hope slipping through my fingers like sand, even as I clung to it desperately.

At fourteen, she had a gun pointed at her inside a busy local mall. She stood frozen as she watched a friend assaulted and bleeding on the floor. That kind of terror imprints itself on a person's soul.

She still didn't know how to form healthy relationships, but somehow, everyone who met her could sense she was an extraordinary human being.

At fifteen, she was taken from my home in handcuffs. Even then, she would cry and apologize, telling me she didn't understand why she treated me so badly and desperately wanted to do better.

By sixteen, she had moved in with birth cousins and was immersed in a dangerous world of drinking, drug use, and unsafe sexual situations. She was drinking vodka before school and smoking weed all day, every day.

And then, at seventeen, she came to me with a request that cracked my heart wide open. "I want to come home," she said. And of course,

I welcomed her back, with open arms but also with boundaries, because both of us needed them.

A few weeks later, she came to me again and said, "I haven't smoked weed in two days and I feel awful, but I want to quit." I offered to get medication to help ease the withdrawal, but she shook her head. "No. I want to feel this, so I never do it again." In that moment, hope was reborn.

What followed was a season of healing, for her and for us. After years of chaos, we began to rebuild our relationship. The bond we forged in that time felt like a miracle, something we had both fought for with everything we had.

But life wasn't finished testing her.

After two years of sobriety, the universe unleashed a new hell. Her birth father died from fentanyl poisoning, a devastating blow that could have shattered her progress. The grief was overwhelming, the pain unrelenting.

Yet she stayed sober. She kept showing up for herself and for her future.

I worked tirelessly to support her emotionally, meeting her where she was and letting her lead the way. Each time she told me I was her best friend, my heart swelled with gratitude. Each time she achieved something once thought impossible, pride poured from my very pores. Hope for her future became not just a flicker but a steady flame.

Through it all, I've learned my job is not to "fix" her but to help her build a sense of self-worth, to show her, over and over again, that there is no shame in her story. To love her relentlessly, not as a reward but as a constant, so that even in her darkest moments, she would know she is worthy.

Our journey hasn't been linear. It has been messy, heartbreaking, beautiful, and redemptive. It is the story of a child who began life with trauma in her veins but fought for her own healing. It is the story of a mother who learned that love alone isn't enough, but that love combined with advocacy, persistence, and grace can change everything.

And above all, it is a story of resilience. Hers, mine, and ours together.

"It took a lot of women like that, a lot of women who said "I'm not going to do what you expect me to do, because you have no idea what I'm capable of. I'm going to get dirty and use tools and live the way I want" to move the world forward."
~Maureen Johnson~

THE WHISPER BEFORE THE STORM
HEATHER MULLEN

I Thought I Knew Who I Was

Before cancer, I was many things, daughter, wife, friend, chameleon. I lived for applause and approval, woven from others' expectations, stitched with a threadbare sense of self. I had mastered the performance. I was who they needed me to be. I did what was acceptable, applauded. I kept myself hidden in plain sight.

To my mother, I was her emotional caretaker. In many ways, I became her mother, holding her feelings like glass, making sure nothing shattered. Love, I learned, was conditional: given for soothing, fixing, pleasing. I wore that truthlike skin, not knowing I could shed it.

She wasn't a bad person. She carried her own disconnection like an inheritance she never asked for. She didn't mean to place me in that role, but she did. This isn't blame. It's truth, wrapped in compassion.

Beneath all that, I was my own harshest judge, scrutinizing every word, curve, and pore. My voice too masculine, my lips too full, my freckles too many. I carried the weight of my body like a private shame. I dressed to hide or to please, never to celebrate the temple I walked in.

Intimacy was a theater of its own. I didn't want to be seen, not truly. I avoided mirrors, avoided light. My body wasn't something to be adored. It was something to be endured.

By twenty, I'd had three major surgeries. People called me strong, but it wasn't strength, it was disconnection. I had dulled myself to pain. My nervous system had gone dim. I wore suffering like a badge, hoping it made me worthy, good, enough.

There were times I silenced my body the way a mother hushes a screaming child, not out of cruelty, but fear. Be quiet. Don't disturb the peace. But it was my own peace I feared breaking.

Once, during my divorce, I even turned pain inward. Not to die, but to feel something. The emotional wound was invisible, so I made it visible. Just once. But it marked me.

I longed for faith but couldn't find a shape that fit. I wandered in and out of churches, sometimes curious, sometimes desperate. There were moments of stillness, flickers of connection. But peace was always followed by judgment. I wanted a God within, not above. Communion, not performance. A place where no one was shamed or "lesser."

But Catholic guilt clung like fog. Even when I stopped going, I still prayed. in fear, in confusion. Something in me knew there was more. A whisper: You are not alone. I didn't yet realize the one listening might have been me.

Those years, I lived as two people: the one I thought I should be, and the one buried beneath shame and silence.

I dismissed the rectal bleeding that persisted for a year. Told myself it was just hemorrhoids. That's how numb I was, ignoring fatigue, iron deficiency, exhaustion.

Pain had become normal. I wasn't just ignoring symptoms. I was ignoring me.

Somewhere, I decided that finding myself would only lead to pain. Each attempt had met rejection or misunderstanding. So, I stopped reaching. I survived instead.

My life became a script.

At family barbecues, I was the Accomplished One, listing achievements like poems I didn't believe. With friends, the Complainer. At parties, the Smiling Mask. The Perfect Daughter. The Good Catholic. The Strong One.

But each time I played a role, something in me tightened. A heaviness in my chest. A lump in my stomach. I knew I was pretending. And pretending hurt. But to stop meant facing the void beneath the performance, and I wasn't sure I'd survive what lived there.

So, I numbed.

The numbness came in waves: first as fewer tears, then silence, then alcohol, then meaningless intimacy. Long nights with others just as lost, just as broken. It felt easier that way. Safer. But it wasn't living, only survival in disguise.

Even then, my spirit never left me. She hovered above, unseen, watching me forget my own light. If she could've spoken, she'd have said, I'm still here. Even when you can't feel me. Even when you don't believe you're worth finding again.

She knew this unraveling was sacred. She knew the reunion, body and spirit, would shake the ground.

If I drew a map of who I was before cancer, it would be a stage. I was a servant in the wings, never the star, never the villain, never myself. A woman shaped by others' scripts.

Yet there were moments, small glimmers, when I caught sight of my own light. They kept me alive. Kept a tether. Kept me close enough to hear the scream when it came. Because some people never do.

Even when I was numb and fading, I was still listening, not with ears, but with ache. The tension in my jaw, the exhaustion in my bones, the grief that lived behind my ribs, it was all my body, trying to speak. I just didn't know the language.

My body had become the battleground for everything I didn't know how to say. She held the shame, the questions, the pain. She spoke through migraines, fatigue, and chaos, and I silenced her every time. Yet beneath that, there was always a flicker.

Even in numbness, even in laughter that wasn't real, even lying beside someone who didn't see me, I saw myself, just for a second. Long enough to feel the whisper: This isn't it.

That flicker, that ember, is why I heard the scream when it finally came. Some call it disease, tragedy, fate. But I knew it as a summoning. I didn't yet know the path, but I knew it wasn't the end. Some part of me, my soul, had always known I'd have to fall apart to come home.

Looking back now, I don't hate the girl I was, the one who performed, stayed quiet, wore invisibility like armor. I honor her. She protected me the only way she knew how. She never stopped trying to remember.

She whispered prayers into the dark even when she doubted anyone was listening. She swallowed grief, told jokes instead. She filled the roles, daughter, Catholic, good girl, party girl, strong one. But underneath, she was always watching for light.

Even the smallest beam through stage curtains, she noticed. Even when surrounded by sadness, she could still feel birdsong in her bones. Even when she thought she was lost, she was laying the bread-crumb trail home.

There was always a quiet pulse beneath the numbness. A golden thread. A flicker of wild. A breath that didn't belong to this world, and it stayed.

There's a holiness in the time before the unraveling, a sacred hush before the thunder cracks open the sky. Before cancer, before I knew what would be asked of me, I lived in a fog of forgetting. But that fog was not failure. It was fermentation, a long, aching alchemical sleep so the awakening would mean something.

Part of me had to forget who I was, so I could remember it as mine, not something inherited or performed.

The ache of disconnection became the drumbeat of my return. Every act of self-abandonment carried a thread back home. Every time I silenced my truth, it grew louder. Every time I looked in the mirror and saw shame, my soul whispered, Still, I am here.

And she was. Always.

Even when I called her gone.

Even when I forgot I was sacred.

I had to live the illusion to break it.

And in those final days before the scream, before the diagnosis, before the portal blew open, I was not asleep. I was gathering.

And the girl I used to be?

She wasn't weak.

She wasn't blind.

She was brave enough to hold the ache until I was ready to meet it.

"One woman filled with self love and self acceptance is a model more super than any cover girl.
~Amy Leigh Mercree~

HER TEXT HAD READ

JULIE TRAINER

Her Text Had Read,

"I found out why I've been having this tummy ache," paired with a sad Bitmoji. Just days earlier, she'd sent a Bitmoji holding balloons that said, "Happy New Year, I hope 2020 will be a great year for us all." "I'll take time off work and care for you," I reassured her. "Oh honey, don't do that just yet. I still feel like me," she insisted, always putting my needs first. Something told me not to wait. I booked a Valentine's Day flight and planned to stay through her first chemo.

I watched mom prepare for bed the first night of my visit. After brushing her teeth at the kitchen sink, she stood at the stove, touching each burner knob three times. "I know, I'm OCD," she explained. "But this is how I've kept the house from burning down all these years." My heart flooded with compassion.

She truly believed her rituals kept us safe, and the cost of her worries was stage four pancreatic cancer. She looked small and frail now. I felt death creeping in around her edges when we hugged. We tried to enjoy simple things, coffee runs, shopping, laughter, but the toll was visible.

Despite her oncologist's warning that "Chemo is a long shot, but it could buy you time," we proceeded. She had port surgery first, which weakened her further. One week later, I held her hand as the infusion slowly filled her veins.

When her cancer markers skyrocketed, she stopped chemo and Dr. Chan suggested hospice. My brother objected.

"Doesn't hospice mean you're giving up?"

But after a week of driving her to the hospital for fluids while she vomited in the car, I called hospice anyway.

Meeting our hospice team felt oddly celebratory.

Mom and Dad shared stories of their 60-year marriage, and I saw them with fresh eyes as the newlyweds they had once been, bravely moving to Los Angeles from their small town in Ohio. I breathed a sigh of relief. Medications, equipment, and reassurance would now come to us regularly.

Then the pandemic lockdown began. Everyone thought it would last a week or two, until restaurants shut down, flights were canceled, store shelves emptied, and mom's friends stopped visiting. Even worse, hospice visits shifted to phone calls.

I left the guest room at my brother's house and moved into my childhood bedroom with my daughter, where we would share an air mattress for the next three months. We removed furniture, boxes, books, and kitchen clutter to make the spaces functional.

"Please let me know where you put things so I can find them later," she said, watching us.

"Sure Mom," we said, letting her believe in a future where she might cook again.

We became her cooks, nurses, and death doulas.

My father remained stubbornly unhelpful, the TV blaring even when Mom begged, "I'm tired of hearing the daily Covid death toll." Each morning it became harder for her to endure the pain of cancer spreading through her body.

"Whenever I wake up, I'm disappointed," she said quietly.

As the pain and medication increased, her abilities decreased. Death was certain but the days were unpredictable. She resisted changing her daily routine, trying to hold on to "normal." But it became harder to accommodate her wishes as the 800 sq. ft. house became too big for her to navigate. With doorways too small for a wheelchair, we had to support her every step. I barely caught her one night while helping her shower. It was becoming dangerous.

Then one night, the fall happened. From a dead sleep, I heard my father yelling, "Can you move your legs?"

I leapt out of bed to find him outside the bathroom, while inside her body was wedged against the door.

"Mom, are you okay?" I called. "No answer, just a soft moan conveying pain and fear."

"Try to move your legs!" my father shouted.

"I don't think she can," I said, panic rising. Nicole rushed in. "Grandma, it's Nicole. I need to get in there to help you." When my father pushed harder on the door, she stopped him.

"You're going to hurt her! Go sit down and let us handle this!"

To my amazement, he did. She had no fear of this old man who once terrorized me and my brother. I flashed back to being four, watching my father pull my brother from under the bed and beat him with a belt. As he blotted my brother's welts afterwards, I had tried to open this very bathroom door to help, but he'd shouted, "Go on, or you'll get the same thing!"

I obeyed, powerless. Now, decades later, I watched my strong daughter squeeze through the narrow opening and lift her grandmother off the floor. "She bumped her head, and she's confused." Nicole said. "I'm calling hospice," I said.

"No!" my father barked. "What the hell do you need to call them for?" "Because she fell and that's what you do when someone is in hospice!"

My sharp tone and the authority I spoke with surprised me. For the first time, I defied him, unconcerned with his response. The power in this house had shifted. Nicole and I were in charge now. I felt strangely empowered.

After settling Mom into bed, she whispered, "Don't leave me. I feel like you're my mommy now, and I don't want to let you out of my sight."

"I'm right here. I won't leave you," I promised. The sacred dance of mother and daughter reversed: she had brought me into this world, and I was helping her leave.

The hospice nurse finally arrived, checked mom's vitals, and said she was ok for now. Then she asked, "Does your dad have a belt?"

I was momentarily speechless at the thought of touching that symbol of my childhood terror. She met my eyes and seemed to understand. "I only ask because sometimes wrapping it around the waist helps steady her movement." I thanked her for the suggestion, knowing I wouldn't use it.

Before leaving, she assured us a hospice bed and portable commode would be delivered in the morning. Nicole and I couldn't sleep after all that.

Covid anxiety had kept her inside for weeks and was turning into agoraphobia. She said, "Let's take a walk, I need to get some cash." So, in the safety of early dawn, we leashed the dog and walked through the empty streets, masks on, bandanas over our faces, and hands gloved to touch the ATM machine.

"In any other time, we'd look like bank robbers," I joked, and she laughed. From a passing car that seemed to float by, I heard Bruce Springsteen crooning

"Even if we're just dancing in the dark."

For a moment, I was transported back to my teenage years when life seemed ordinary, unlike tonight when my dying mother fell, my daughter was a hero, and I stood up to my father.

We were just dancing in the dark with cancer in the middle of a pandemic.

"Just as every human creature needs a place to be alone in, a sacred, private "home" of his own, so all human creatures need a place to be together in, from the two who can show each other their souls uninterruptedly, to the largest throng that can throb and stir in unison.
∼Charlotte Perkins Gilman∼

PHOENIX RISING FROM THE ASHES
CATHERINE CHAPMAN-KING

"Trauma doesn't die with those who lived it. It lingers. It weaves itself
into the double helix, carried forward like an echo."
~Catherine Chapman-King~

Unearthing the Roots For years, I've been a treasure hunter. Not of
gold or jewels, but of something that's far more precious truth. The
truth of where I come from, the people who came before me, and the
shadows that shaped my bloodline.

My digging hasn't been in the dirt with shovels, but in memories,
public records, whispers, and scars. And over and over again, I've
found myself pulled toward my father's side, the biological, fraternal,
Indigenous side of my family.

It has been no gentle journey to say the least. What I've unearthed is
jagged and raw: a horrific past, disturbing truths buried deep under
silence, pain swept beneath the carpet for generations.

But this search is not for them. Not for recognition. Not for history books. I do it for me. For the little girl who was taken away before she had words to ask why.

I was only eighteen months old when I was taken from my parents. The separation is one of my earliest scars, an absence branded on my soul. Children's Aid placed me into a foster home, one of the worst in Toronto, not because I belonged there, but because they said there was a shortage of homes.

Falstaff Apartments, Toronto housing: hard concrete walls, broken glass, chaos. I lived there for two years, too young to defend myself, old enough to remember the pain.

And then, at three years old, I was given a miracle. I was adopted by Carole and Terry Chapman, two people who showed me what pure love truly meant. They were, and still are, the definition of care, the embodiment of kindness. They were the blessing in disguise that saved me.

If every child had parents like them, this world would not be so broken. I carry endless gratitude for them.

But even in that home filled with love, I felt... different. Alien. As if I didn't belong to this world. My perception of things, my ways of feeling, never seemed to match the others around me. Summers darkened my skin to almost black, winters drained me pale.

People asked if I was Egyptian, Syrian, European. They noticed the wiggle in my walk. They marveled at my eyes, cat-like, sharp, unique, like no one they had ever seen. Many thought I wore contacts but that wasn't so.

At school, we'd do family tree projects. I'd go home and ask my adoptive parents about our history, and I would proudly write down the Chapman lineage. That was my family, too. But biologically, genetically, in the marrow of my bones and the blood of my veins, I knew I belonged elsewhere. I needed to know where.

Years unfolded.

I became a mother of five, three sons, two daughters, and later, a grandmother to ten grandchildren. A family of my own: beautiful, strong.

But alongside the blessings, shadows followed me. Anxiety haunted me like a ghost I couldn't name. Panic would seize me, sometimes so heavy I couldn't breathe. I knew why I flinched at touch, why I resisted affection, hat was the mark of the foster home. But the endless nerves, the racing heart, the sense of dread that never left? That, I couldn't explain.

Life, though, has its strange ways of sending mirrors. After my fifth child, I had my tubes tied. Later, through a friend, I was introduced to a fertility clinic in downtown Toronto. Wanting to give others the gift I had been blessed with; I donated my eggs. Through in vitro fertilization, a woman carried twin boys born of my DNA.

Fate has its quirks. She named one of the boys Jesse, the same name as one of my sons.

Years later, when the boys were around eight, the clinic contacted me. The woman wanted to know my identity. Everything had been anonymous, but her boys had questions in their very being. She wanted answers for them, the kind I had once longed for myself. She wanted to know where their gifts came from.

One boy was extremely artistic, drawn to the piano. Neither she nor her husband had an artistic bone. But I did. He also suffered from anxiety, the same anxiety I had lived with all my life. That moment was a revelation. My struggles were not just mine, they were threads of inheritance, passed down through DNA.

And suddenly, I understood trauma doesn't die with those who lived it. It lingers. It weaves itself into the double helix, carried forward like an echo.

My grandmother, locked away in a reformatory, brutalized, broken, left scars that reached me generations later. The abuse, the fear, the resilience, it lived in me. And I, unknowingly, passed it on.

That truth changed everything. It made me dig deeper, not just into names and records, but into who I am. Into the wounds of my ancestors, into the patterns that repeat, into the darkness and into the light.

I am not just unearthing history. I am unearthing myself. For me. For my children. For my grandchildren. For the future. To understand that we are not just shaped by what we live through here and now, but by what those before us endured. To know that pain can travel but so can healing.

And so, my treasure hunt continues.

Everything is within your power,
and your power is within you."
~Janice Trachtman~

BLOOMING WILD

SABRINA LAMBERT

Being born in the latter half of the 1950s meant growing up surrounded by rules, both unspoken and overt, for girls. The expectations around how we behaved, dressed, and even how we were to feel about things were very rigid and compliance was socialized much more than it is today.

I grew up in a household where my mother, a schoolteacher, was less publicly emotional than my father. He had no qualms about showing sadness, anger, or joy. I remember him crying when I was little, something I never saw my mother do. It's interesting how emotion seemed reversed in my home.

Men could express it, women restrained it. It wasn't until I was an adult, and my own mom's wild woman started to bloom that I saw her tears. I was more open with my own daughter, letting her see me and how it was ok to express feelings.

Yet, our childhood dinner table was a place for open conversation. We could talk about anything, such as school happenings, current events, and what it meant to be kind. It was at that table that I learned to be curious and thoughtful.

Still, the lesson outside our home was clear: "Good girls" didn't make a scene. We were taught that our behaviour reflected on our parents. We, their children, were living proof of their success or failure.

So, I followed the rules. I kept my room clean, my marks high, and my emotions tempered. I was friendly, likable, and never a problem child. The wild woman in me, the one that exists in all girls, was quiet, hibernating, and waiting.

However, wild things do not remain dormant forever.

Having the opportunity to attend University in the late 1970's created cracks in my perfect good girl persona. I was suddenly surrounded by possibility, new ideas, people from other cultures, and glimpses of what freedom could look like. During my first year, I dated a man eleven years my senior and I failed my first political science essay. We'd been out celebrating my honors award, partied hard, and stayed out until dawn.

It was my first failed grade in my life. But it didn't feel like failure. It was my first hint that living can teach us more than red marks on a forgotten term paper ever could.

During summer breaks, I worked to pay tuition. I remember one job interview vividly. A bare room containing only two chairs amplified the interview questions that made my skin prickle. The man's undertone was unmistakable. He looked at me as if I were an accessory to the position, and not a mind with skills to be valued. I left knowing I would never work for him.

It was early in the 1980s when a majority of women were entering the workforce, yet the old biases lingered. Men were hired for potential; women were judged for their looks, age, and likelihood of leaving to have babies. It becomes easy to see how self-doubt took root for so many of us back then.

Yet, I was successfully hired full-time by a national airline, due to my accuracy skills and attention to details. I loved the work. The technical challenge, the people, the problem-solving was all intellectually and socially stimulating. The big bonus, I could travel the world.

Three years in, I ran into an old teacher. When I told him what I did, he frowned.

"You could do more," he said. "Be a doctor or lawyer."

He meant it kindly, but I remember thinking whose definition of 'more' is the most important?

That job became my 39-year career. It fulfilled me in ways status never could. I worked with the public, trained others, and then led a large team, learning constantly. Eventually, the leadership workload also burned me out and made me ill, however even that taught me lessons I needed to learn.

As women in the 80s and 90s, we were told, "You can have it all"

Maybe we could, however I believe it cannot be had all at the same time. Balance isn't about equal time at work and home. I believe that it's about balancing energy in how you choose to spend it.

I learned that energy needs to be spent where I need it the most. Some days it is on rest and recuperation, other days it is spent on productivity and creativity, and many days it's spent on doing things I love with the people I love. Although I learned the hard way, I know it was the most valuable lesson of my life.

For years, I thought having emotions was a weakness or something to control. But feeling emotions, I learned, is really part of my own data loop.

In my twenties and thirties, I was often on a roller coaster of feelings. Eventually, as I got older, I realized my emotions followed my thoughts. If I could pause, reflect, and choose the thoughts I believed, I could feel fully without being consumed or be seen as losing it. That awareness gave me sovereignty over my reactions.

Still, being an emotional woman carried stigma.

Two memories have stuck with me. First, when I was in the hospital giving birth, my blood pressure was dangerously high. Doctors and nurses whispered around me, telling my husband and parents what was happening but did not include me, fearing that I'd "get upset" and further exacerbate my condition.

Months later, I told my doctor, "Being emotional doesn't make me irrational. I can always make a decision given the pertinent information."

Then, many years later at work as a manager, I cried in frustration over an unfair corporate directive. My male supervisor said, "There's no crying in leadership."

I looked him straight in the eye, and told him, "This is how I process frustration. You still like the results I deliver, right? Then this is part of the package."

I wasn't apologizing for my emotions anymore. They do not show weakness. They were my truth, my authenticity.

As I aged, the world started treating me differently. People could misjudge my age, sometimes younger, sometimes older and that often seemed as if it determined my worth.

Over time, I stopped chasing youth. Coloring my hair until it started to fall out, painting my nails, hiding my face with makeup, it all felt like a performance. When I stopped, my hair, nails, and skin thanked me. More importantly, I felt more like me. I felt comfortable in my own skin.

No longer performing womanhood, I was simply being a woman.

I wasn't striving to be youthful, but I was choosing to live with presence.

Society tends to call women like me "crones." I smile. To me, that's a title of wisdom and earned experience. I'm no longer performing, I'm living presence with empathy, insight, and grace.

Once I walked along the sidewalks near my home. The air was crisp, while the sunlight was soft and warm on my face. I paused to breathe, noticing the quiet strength in my body that's been through decades of striving, mothering, healing, learning.

My reflection in a picture window of a woman with silver hair flying loose in the breeze, caught my eye. She smiled, and I waved back in a silent recognition. We made it. We're still here, still growing, living unapologetically wild.

That wild woman who once slept within me, has awakened. She's thriving. She's my intuition, my courage, my laughter, and my presence.

Women boomers are not fading away, we are blooming. We're redefining our own vision of womanhood with our own rules.

Looking back, I see each persona, the good girl, the seeker, the leader, and the mother as my evolution toward authenticity.

Today, I am unapologetically emotional, intuitive, and alive. I trust my intuition. I am worthy by just being. I live aligned with my energy. I no longer need approval to feel deeply or to rest deeply.

My wild woman has been with me on every path. She was using this time to bloom. Now, she's blossomed, finally visible, finally free to be who she is, and ready for whatever comes next.

"You just have to say to yourself, "I am not willing to accept anything less than what I deserve! I am smart! I am Beautiful! I am a good woman, and I deserve to be happy!"
It all starts with you."
~Amari Soul~

Cats and Dildos from Now On

You feel entitled,
Want me to cheerlead you,
Give you my pedestal,
Hold you on my shoulders,
While I sink into the mud.

Wading through muck for us both,
Keeping your feet clean,
As you look down, breathing your fresh air,
Disgusted by how stagnant I've become.

Your feet get muddy, you notice,
my mouth is barely above ground,
I can take us no further.

If you weren't so useless,
you'd save yourself and let me drown.

You want me to listen not speak,
unless it's to grovel, compliment or stroke.

You question me at my core,
Explain things I already know,
Dismissing, not caring, when I explicitly say so:
"Yeah, but let me tell you anyway."

Bro, I have ADHD,
You're torturing my soul,
I know what a _____ is,
how that works,
where this story goes.

54

I'm not your audience,
Your validation,
Your anything at all.

I am mine, my own, my precious,
Not ruled by your ego,
I'm not here to fit into your life,
stand in your shadow,
facilitate your dreams,
Nothing at the expense of my own.

Cats and dildos from now on.

Maybe someone will come along,
I want to share myself with,
We can enjoy each other,
our experiences,
Hold space with kindness and warmth.

I belong to me,
clear and clean,
Always have,
forever will.

- Erin Fairweather

"She will blaze through you like a gypsy wildfire. Igniting you soul and dancing in its flames. And when she is gone, the smell of her smoke will be the only thing left to soothe you."
~Nicole Lyons~

I DID NOT ENJOY BEING PREGNANT! - IT FELT ALIEN, ODD, ICKY AND GROSS.

ARLEEN DAVIS

On April 11, 2002, I came home early from work feeling sick. I felt flush, dizzy, nauseous with a mild headache. My husband came home and was going to sort out dinner.

I told him with no uncertainty. "I am not hungry and do not want to eat," "Go get yourself something." I kindly suggested. He agreed and was heading out the door when I had a sudden craving for KFC.

"Honey! I really want KFC." I yelled out.

"WHAT?" He replied in confusion. We never ate Kentucky Fried Chicken.

"You want KFC?" he asked with surprise.

"I do." I confirmed. "Ok. What do you want exactly?" he lovingly asked.

My husband came back with chicken and a pregnancy test. His intuition was correct. I was pregnant.

We were both very excited and celebrated the news. We spent the rest of the evening talking about how to tell the future grandparents, names for the baby to be, when to see the doctor, and when to tell our employers and friends. It was all a bit overwhelming.

Fast forward four months when my abdomen started to be noticeably larger and my clothes needed adjusting. I started to feel less like myself and more like someone with a thing growing inside of them. It felt awkward. No matter how much I exercised or stretched my body appeared to do what it wanted. I was not used to this, and I did not like it.

At six months I started experiencing indigestion and heartburn. I was on track for weight gain, with an ever-growing abdomen and butt. On the outside I felt honoured to be a part of the "Mother to Be Club," but on the inside was confusion and discomfort.

I was experiencing intermittent mild diarrhea and constipation, mild cramping and bloating. The doctor suggested it was normal in pregnancy. It just put me on alert for nearby bathrooms and possible flatulence getaway areas, making me feel more uncomfortable, alien and gross.

I had started to struggle to get up stairs, waddled around like an over-sized penguin trying my best to hold it together.

Whenever someone would ask about the pregnancy I replied with the standard, "Everything is going great. The baby is growing as expected." But, when someone reached out to touch my growing abdomen, I flinched. Instinctively, I would try to suck it in, but that was impossible. It left me feeling defenseless and embarrassed.

The social expectations made me feel more uncomfortable than expected, but what I was feeling inside surprised me more. As the baby moved and stretched, I thought of the movie Alien. I had this baby pushing its body around inside of me, forming shapes on my abdomen that were creeping me out, and I honestly could barely touch it.

I want to be excited and rest my hand on my belly and feel joy and warmth as other moms did. However, I often flinched when I felt or saw the head, hand or foot push or move across my abdomen. It reminded me of the movie.

At eight months I experienced an increase of constipation with pain. The doctor did a quick rectal exam and found hemorrhoids. It was not surprising. She recommended rest with a high fiber diet.

I had gained 35 pounds during the pregnancy and still had a month to go with two weeks of work before my maternity leave started. She was concerned for the size of the baby. I was concerned about my size and my bowels.

December 12, 2002, I was at work and invited to join the community outing to the bowling center. Although I felt uncomfortable and huge, I thought it would be an easy afternoon on my last day of work. Being young and a bit bull headed, I decided to throw a few balls. I went home with cramps in my abdomen and back, the beginning of what turned out to be labour.

At 6:00 pm that evening the camps started coming every 10 minutes.

"Should we go to the hospital?" my husband asked worriedly.

"No, not yet. We were told to go when they were 5 minutes apart." I told him reassuringly.

I was not going any earlier than I had to and I was not ready to make this baby come out of my vagina.

I went to bed at 11:00 pm with mild contractions seven minutes apart. I laid there wondering how this was going to play out. Would I get some sleep tonight before I went into labour? Then I heard a loud POPPING sound in my head.

"What the heck was that?"

I noticed that my husband did not react. I got out of bed to check and felt the gush. My water broke. Here we go!

"Honey, honey! You need to get up. My water just broke!" I said as calmly as possible.

What?' He yelled, stumbling out of bed.

"What do I need to do?" He asked scurrying around the bedroom to get his clothes.

"Grab the hospital bag and go start the truck." I calmly told him.

It was December in Ontario; it was -5 Celsius.

At the hospital I walked the halls and bounced on a yoga ball to further the dilation for several hours. The contractions felt no worse than bad period cramps. That ended abruptly!

When it was time to push all, I felt was the baby's weight. I did not know how to push. OH! I was also too late for pain medicine, other than the nitrous oxide that wears off quickly.

Pushing for an hour only resulted in the baby crowning and getting stuck. I could do no more. They discussed forceps to which I groggily yelled "Please, no!"

A suction device was administered and after 10 minutes of excruciating pain Anna was born. My husband cut the umbilical cord. Anna was weighed and then placed on my chest. She still felt like an alien, and I struggled to feel joy in that moment.

My story was not done.

It was time for the placenta to be birthed. Upon that adventure I hemorrhaged. What I recall was feeling the life force leaving me, drained from the tip of my head downward as the bed tilted back. As blood spouted from my vagina and doctors discussed transferring me to a critical care hospital, I thought, "Don't leave my baby here."

Fortunately, the doctors acted quickly. They said most red haired, blue eyed and pale skinned mothers hemorrhaged giving birth. With a heavy iron rich diet, my bloods returned to almost normal, and I was released after five days with iron supplements.

Unfortunately, this led to further bowel complications that four months later I discovered were the beginnings of what I would be diagnosed with in April 2003; Ulcerative Colitis.

It took me months to properly bond with Anna. Not only did I feel awkward, uncomfortable and alien during pregnancy and birth, I had an underlying disease awakening inside that took my attention away from being a mom for the first six months of my first child's life.

"The strength of a woman is not measured by the impact that all her hardships in life have had on her; but the strength of a woman is measured by the extent of her refusal to allow those hardships to dictate her and who she becomes."
~C. JoyBell.C.~

WILD HORSES, WILD WOMAN
TRISH SCHOULAR

All my life, people have said I remind them of wild horses, galloping, untamed, impossible to fence in. At first, I didn't know what they meant. But now I see it: there is something in me that has never tolerated being controlled, silenced, or told which way to run.

I grew up believing, like many girls, that by the time I was twenty-five I would be married. I even remember someone giving me a cup and saucer, a not-so-subtle suggestion that I might end up an "old maid." But I never saw myself that way. I was attractive, sweet, kind, fun. Still, in the church and in my friendships, I often felt overlooked.

I remember liking a man once, only to find out later that a friend had kept me away from him because she wanted him with her friend, who eventually married him. That kind of betrayal cut deep.

Other times, I'd share that I was interested in someone, and people would laugh: "Oh, he probably has three or four others." I can still feel the sting of that. Why didn't they want someone like me? I couldn't understand it.

And yet, despite all that, I've come to see the truth: I don't need rescuing. I don't need a man to give me worth or to make my life feel full. Would it be wonderful to have a partner who could truly match me, to share love and maybe even share the weight of the bills? Of course. But I no longer place my worth in whether a man chooses me. That dream, that myth, is not the one that defines me anymore.

Instead, I define myself. I've learned that being a wild woman is not about waiting for someone to hand you the life you deserve, it's about building it with your own two hands, with your own fierce heart.

Yes, sometimes I attracted the wounded men, the ones carrying heartbreak from ex-wives or broken childhoods. I thought maybe I was meant to heal them. But too often, it only left me hurting, questioning who I was.

I'll never forget a hypnotherapy session I had years ago in Nanaimo, where I was told to hand back what I'd been carrying for others. One by one, I gave back the burdens, and they turned into wounded children. That moment showed me that all my life, I had been holding pain that wasn't mine to hold.

And so, I gave it back. I set it down. I let my wild self return.

The wild woman in me doesn't apologize for wanting more. She doesn't wait for a gate to open; she leaps the fence. She doesn't settle for being tamed, she carries her fire into everything she creates. She doesn't need permission, and she doesn't need rescuing.

She was never broken. She was always free.

"There is something incredibly beautiful about a woman, who knows herself, she can't break, she just falls but, in every fall, she rises, past who she was before."
~Tammie Trites~

Hiding in The Dark

My stomach is at an ache, Rock at the bottom..
My thoughts... are coming in as waves... as the tide takes over.
Drowning all other of my emotions.
The speed, the energy, the rush.

As if there is no time to wait
My body is tensing, as I feel frozen.
In the middle of battle and war.
How can I be so cold but my heart so warm?

As I fight for some sense of knowing.
I desperately hold onto a thin thread.
A thread of old, a thread of... me!
The only piece that could bring me back.
When I slip...

The darkness is so bright!
Blinding and controlling,
a force so familiar and comforting,
but so dangerous and deceiving

All sounds are familiar but unfriendly,
I'm cautious but eager
The texture is rough the pain is real,
A sense of loss is so near

-Rhonda Funk

"Wild woman are an unexplainable spark of life. They ooze freedom and seek awareness; they belong to nobody but themselves yet give a piece of who they are to everyone they meet. "
~Nikki Rowe~

MY DRIVING EXPERIENCE
TAMMIE TRITES

"I wasn't shaped by perfection; I was created through my stories. The
pain, the chaos, the healing, every piece of it
built the woman I am today"
~Tammie Trites~

Looking back, I realize that my introduction to driving wasn't a rite of
passage like it is for most kids. There was no proud moment of getting
a learner's permit, no eager countdown to a 16th birthday. For me,
driving was born out of necessity, born out of chaos, and born far too
early.

My mom worked as a pilot car driver for my father's trucking
company. I was just a kid, probably seven or eight, when I first
learned to shift gears in a small Honda. The memory is blurry around
the edges, but what's vivid is why it happened.

My mom's arm had been run over by my dad. Whether it was intentional or not, I still don't know. That question has lingered in my
mind for years, unanswerable and uncomfortable. But the result was
clear, she couldn't shift the gears anymore.

So, she taught me.

I'd sit in the passenger seat beside her, legs too short to reach the pedals, hands barely big enough to wrap around the stick.

She'd drive, and when it was time to shift, she'd say, "Now."

And I'd do it. Just like that. The mechanics of it didn't make sense to me then, but the rhythm did. It was something primal, instinctual. I wasn't learning how to drive; I was learning how to help my mother survive.

That was my first driving lesson.

It became normal, in a strange kind of way. I didn't realize it was unusual; I didn't know that other kids weren't shifting gears on high-ways before they lost their baby teeth. That experience formed one of my earliest core memories, though at the time, I had no idea how significant it would become.

But the next experience, I knew in the moment that it was going to stick with me forever. It wasn't just unusual. It was terrifying.

I must have still been eight. My mom came to pick me up after one of my drum and bugle corps practices. She was driving a van that could've easily been cast as the getaway vehicle in a horror film, dingy, rusted, and more than a little ominous. The moment I stepped inside, my stomach dropped. I could tell something wasn't right.

She tried to talk, but her words didn't sound like hers. They were slurred, slow, heavy. I didn't fully understand what being drunk meant back then, but I knew what it felt like to sit next to someone who wasn't safe to drive.

We waited in the parking lot until everyone else had left. I think she didn't want anyone to see us. Eventually, she turned to me and said she needed my help. I had to stick my head out the passenger window and tell her when she was close to the ledge of the road. She couldn't see clearly enough herself.

So, there I was. A little girl hanging halfway out the window, calling out directions like some kind of makeshift co-pilot. "Left! No, to the right! Okay, hold it there!"

It was only a seven-minute drive. But it felt like hours. Every second was soaked in anxiety. I was hyper-aware of every bump in the road, every curve, every sound the tires made. I didn't feel brave. I felt trapped. Responsible. Afraid.

That night left a mark. Not just because of the danger, but because of the shift that took place inside me. I wasn't just a child anymore. I had become a silent partner in her secrets. A co-conspirator in keeping everything looking normal from the outside, while inside, nothing was.

As the years passed, the weight of that responsibility only grew heavier.

By the time I was ten, my parents had separated. My mother was with someone new, someone who shared her taste for escape, for recklessness disguised as adventure. They loved going on sponta-neous trips to the United States. They'd shop, hit the bars, and then crash by the ocean in their camper van, sleeping off the alcohol like it was part of the plan.

One day, they invited me to join them. We had friends in Birch Bay, and the idea of getting out of town sounded like a break from the usual. So, I said yes.

We spent the day grocery shopping, wandering the mall, and heading toward the beach. For a little while, it felt like a normal family outing. Like maybe things were okay.

But when I met back up with them at Bellis Fair Mall, everything changed.

They were drunk. Completely out of it. I'd only been gone for three hours, but in that time, they'd downed enough to lose control of their bodies and their judgment. I panicked. I started yelling, crying, screaming at them. "How could you do this to me?" I demanded. "Why would you bring me here and do this?"

And that's when my mother, barely able to keep her balance, looked at me and said the words that still echo in my memory:

"Well, I guess you're really goanna have to put all your driving experience to use, because you have to drive us home."

I froze.

I was thirteen. I had never properly driven a car. I didn't know the rules of the road, the laws, or how to handle turns, signals, traffic. I wasn't a driver. I was a child. But in that moment, none of that seemed to matter to her.

They were too far gone. I begged them not to make me do it. I was terrified. But my mom shrugged and said she had to work in the morning, and that somehow made it final.

So, I drove.

My hands were trembling on the wheel, my eyes constantly darting between the road and the mirrors, my heart pounding so hard I could barely hear my own thoughts. I don't remember much of the route, only the feeling. The pressure. The overwhelming need to be perfect, to not mess up, because the consequences felt so much bigger than me.

I remember trying to stay calm on the outside while my insides were screaming. I couldn't afford to crash. I couldn't afford to cry. I had to hold it together, because nobody else would.

That drive changed something in me. It wasn't just the physical act of driving; it was what it represented. I had crossed a line that kids shouldn't have to cross. I had stepped into the role of protector, of navigator, of the adult.

And they didn't even thank me. It was just expected. Like it was normal.

But it wasn't normal.

These driving experiences weren't about learning independence or preparing for adulthood. They were about survival. About being placed in impossible situations and somehow making it through.

I didn't grow into a confident driver from these moments, I grew into a cautious, anxious one. One who triple-checks the mirrors, who can't stand being a passenger, who still sometimes hears a voice say, "Now," when I shift gears.

I know now that none of that was okay. That no child should be placed in those situations. That it wasn't my job to keep adults safe or get them home. But back then, I didn't have the language or the understanding. I only had the instinct to survive, to protect, and to adapt.

And that's what I did.

I adapted.

That's what children of chaos do. We become whatever we need to be in order to get through. We carry burdens that aren't ours, drive roads we were never ready for, and find ways to smile while doing it. But the weight never leaves, not really. It settles somewhere in the bones.

Even now, when I drive alone down a quiet road, I sometimes feel that little girl in the passenger seat again. The one who had her head out the window, calling out directions. The one who learned too young how to steer through fear.

The one who never had a choice.

Sometimes I think about what that little girl would say to me now if she could. Maybe she'd be proud that I made it out, that I didn't let the chaos define who I became. Or maybe she'd just be tired. I think she'd tell me she's glad I finally learned to pull over, to rest, to let someone else take the wheel for once.

It took years to unlearn the feeling that everything depended on me. That I had to control every moment, every turn, every outcome. It's hard to explain to people why letting someone else drive still makes my chest tighten.

They don't understand that for me, being a passenger once meant danger, uncertainty, and helplessness.

But healing is strange, it doesn't come all at once. It sneaks in through small things. Like realizing I can drive somewhere without panic. Like laughing in the car with my kids, the music up, and no fear in my throat. Those are the moments that feel like freedom to me.

Sometimes my daughters ask why I'm so nervous when they start to drive. I tell them it's just because I love them, but deep down, it's more than that. It's because I know too well how fragile a life can be behind a wheel. How quickly safety can turn into survival.

But they're gentle drivers. Patient. Kind. And when I see that, I know the cycle broke somewhere along the line. That all the fear, the control, the lessons learned in chaos, somehow turned into caution, empathy, and care in them.

I like to believe that's the good that came out of all the hard. That maybe all those nights of fear planted something better in the next generation.

So now, when I drive, I still check the mirrors three times, but I also breathe. I remind myself that I'm not that scared little girl anymore.

I'm the woman who survived her, who carries her, but also who learned how to let her rest.

And for the first time in a long time, the road ahead doesn't just look like survival, it looks like peace.

"Be yourself; everyone else is already taken."
~Oscar Wilde~

THE MAKING OF A WILD WOMAN
JULIE FAIRHURST

I didn't believe I was a wild woman at first. To me, wild sounded reckless, defiant, out of control. But when I began writing about my life, really writing, I discovered that wildness was never about chaos. It was about truth. It was the part of me that refused to stay small, even when the world told me to.

Wildness, I've learned, is not rebellion; it's remembering. It's the whisper that says, "You were made for more than survival."

As I wrote, I met myself again and again, through all my seasons, through every storm and sunrise. I saw her: the Maiden, the Mother, the Warrior, the Wise Woman, the Mystic, and the Alchemist, all alive in me, all rising together.

The Maiden

I began as the Maiden, curious, open, and unafraid to dream. I was the girl who asked too many questions, who believed in possibilities long before she knew what limits were. That spark never left me. Even in the darkest moments, she whispered, "There's still more waiting for you."

The Mother

Then came motherhood, and with it, a kind of wild I never expected. For twenty-four years, I was a single parent raising three boys. I worked harder than hard, sometimes to the point of breaking, but I was determined to show them what strength looked like.

I chose distance from my dysfunctional family, not out of anger but out of love. I wanted my boys to see a better way to live, to know that love could be steady, not conditional. I taught them to show up, to work for what they wanted, to care for themselves and the people they would one day love. I wasn't just raising boys; I was breaking patterns. I was showing them what resilience looked like in human form.

The Warrior

There were years when I had to fight for peace, for purpose, for the right to stand in my own truth. Life has thrown me into the fire more times than I can count, but each time, I rose. I carried my lessons like armor and my hope like a weapon.

I was a warrior when I forgave my dying mother, sitting by her side with a heart that chose love over bitterness. I was a warrior when I stayed strong for my brother, whose long battle with addiction ended in a hospital room after three strokes. I held his hand, not in judgment but in grace.

And I was a warrior when I dared to begin again, when I stepped onto the stage for the first time to speak to women about courage, when I went on TV to promote my mission, when I stood in front of the world as myself, my voice steady and my heart wide open.

The Mystic

On my 50th birthday, I felt the pull of something larger. I booked a flight to Kenya, alone. It wasn't a vacation; it was a pilgrimage. I went to find myself again.

I walked the red earth, watched the sun rise over the savanna, and realized that the universe had been whispering to me all along: It's time to move in a new direction.

In Kenya, I softened. I let down my guard. I fell in love with the world, with life, with myself.

That journey cracked something open in me and gave birth to Women Like Me, a movement, a mission, a home for truth-telling women.

The Wise Woman

Decades in business, sales, and persuasion taught me how to lead, but it was life, loss, love, motherhood, and truth that taught me how to listen.

Wisdom, I've learned, doesn't shout. It moves quietly, grounded and certain. It knows that healing others often means showing your own scars first. So, I began teaching, guiding, and coaching, not from perfection but from presence.

The Alchemist

Looking back, I see now that every time I stepped up, every time I overcame, every time I loved anyway, I was alchemizing. Turning pain into purpose, fear into freedom, stories into legacy.

There was the night I stopped to help a woman and her baby on a dark highway, acting on instinct, love moving faster than fear. There were countless times I poured myself into others, believing that lifting them was part of lifting myself.

I never thought much of it then; I was just moving through life, doing what needed to be done. But now I see it clearly. Every single act of courage, every risk, every act of love was a page in the story of a wild woman rising.

I didn't know I was one of them, not until I began to tell the truth. But now I see her in every word I write, every woman I meet, every mirror I face. I am her, and she is every woman who has ever dared to rise again and again and again.

Now I am awakened to the real me, not the version that played small to make others comfortable, not the one who tried to fit into roles that never quite fit, but the whole me, the woman I was always meant to become.

With every sunrise, every lesson, every scar and smile, I learn more about who I am, and I love her fiercely. I love the wild woman who refused to give up, the one who worked, who raised, who healed, who dared, the one who never stopped becoming.

I no longer resist her. I no longer tame her. I embrace her, all of her: every wrong turn, every heartbreak, every victory, every fall. There were no mistakes. I was not a mistake. Life was meant to carry me exactly the way it did, through the chaos and the calm, through the fire and the grace.

Every path I walked, even the painful ones, was carved just for me, a sacred trail of becoming.

Each experience, each heartbreak, each triumph, they were not detours; they were directions.

Now I understand, the universe was never against me; it was guiding me. Every storm cleared the debris that blocked my next step. Every loss cracked open a deeper layer of love. Every silence taught me to hear the whispers of my own soul.

So, I ask you, dear sister reading this, examine your life.

Look at the paths you've walked, the choices you've made, the moments when you thought you'd never rise, and yet you did.

Do you listen to the universe as you move forward? Do you hear her calling your name between the chaos and the quiet?

Because she's there, your wild woman, each of the archetypes, the Maiden, the Mother, the Warrior, the Wise Woman, the Mystic, and the Alchemist, lives inside you too. Perhaps you haven't seen her yet. Maybe she's buried beneath old stories, beneath guilt, expectation, fear, or fatigue.

But when you are ready, she will rise. She will push her way to the surface with a roar so fierce it will wake the women around you. They will feel your truth like a spark, and in that moment, something ancient will stir in them, too.

That's how it happens, one woman's awakening becomes another's permission. When you step into your wildness, you give others the courage to do the same. And when we all rise together, the world shifts.

So let her out. Let her roar. Let her dance in the sunlight of her own freedom. The world has waited long enough to meet the woman you were always meant to be.

"I'm not going to do what you expect me to do, because you have no idea what I'm capable of. I'm going to get dirty and use tools and live the way I want to move the world forward."
~Maureen Johnson~

TOLD TO BE QUIET
LAVERNE FELLING

I grew up being told to be quiet.

Apparently, my laugh was too loud, my questions too constant, my emotions too big. I was the child who loved too much, felt too deeply, and wanted too often to be held. To my parents, that was "too much." To me, it was simply me.

But I learned early that being myself was dangerous. That love could vanish if I took up too much space. That affection was conditional on silence. So, I became small.

I learned to tiptoe through life, holding my breath around people who never noticed the effort it took. I trained myself to read moods, to sense tension, to apologize before I even knew what for.

My voice was dimmed into a whisper that only I could hear.

By the time I reached adulthood, I was a master of disappearing. I could sit in a room full of people and be invisible. I could say "yes" when my whole body screamed "no." I could shrink myself down to fit into anyone's expectations, no matter how much it hurt.

And it hurt, a lot.

I let people walk over me. I let employers underpay and overwork me. I let friends drain my energy and lovers define my worth. I confused kindness with compliance and mistook silence for peace.

But beneath all of that quiet, something fierce was waiting. It wasn't gone, it was just buried. My wild woman was still in there, pacing in the dark, waiting for her cue to rise.

That moment came one ordinary afternoon.

I was walking home from work, exhausted from another day of being agreeable. The sun was soft, sinking low over the city, and I remember feeling like life was happening in black-and-white. I existed, but I didn't live.

As I turned the corner onto my street, I saw a family ahead of me, a man, a woman, and a small child, maybe six or seven years old. The little girl had a pink backpack and wild curls, and she was crying. The parents were yelling, their words slicing through the evening air.

"Stop being such a baby!" "Why can't you ever do anything right?"

Each insult landed like a slap, and I froze. My throat tightened. It was like watching my own childhood replay in front of me, scene by scene. That little girl's trembling shoulders mirrored mine from decades before.

Something inside me broke, no, not broke. Snapped awake.

I didn't say anything to them. I just stood there, heart pounding, tears burning in my eyes. But in that moment, something ancient rose up from the ashes inside me. A knowing. A vow.

Never again.

Never again would I let anyone treat me as less than I am.

Never again would I silence myself for someone else's comfort.

Never again would I abandon my own voice.

That was the day my wild woman rose. Not in a loud, dramatic explosion, but in a quiet, unwavering decision to come home to myself.

At first, using my voice felt terrifying. Every "no" trembled on my tongue like a newborn fawn learning to stand. Every boundary I set felt like betrayal. I worried people would leave me, and many did.

But here's what I didn't know then: When you start standing in your truth, only those built to meet you there will stay.

At work, I began to speak up. When a project was unfairly dumped on me, I calmly said, "That's not my responsibility." The first time I did it, my hands shook. But later that night, I slept better than I had in years.

Soon, opportunities started to find me, promotions, projects, recognition. Turns out, when you act like you matter, the world starts to believe you.

With friends, I began noticing who only called when they needed something and who truly cared how I was doing. Some friendships faded quietly. Others exploded when I stopped playing the "people pleaser."

And with men, well, oh, that was a revolution of its own!

I stopped mistaking attention for affection. I stopped confusing attraction with connection. I stopped letting charm override respect. For the first time in my life, I looked at myself in the mirror and said, "You are the prize."

The woman I am now barely recognizes the girl who once whispered apologies for existing.

I speak loudly. I laugh even louder. I cry when I need to and walk away when I must. I don't chase anyone, and I don't beg to be understood.

My boundaries are not walls; they are sacred gates that protect my peace.

And yes, many people have dropped from my life. But here's the truth no one tells you: When you release what no longer aligns, you create space for miracles.

New people entered, women who inspire me, friends who cheer for my growth instead of competing with it, and men who see my strength as something to be honored, not managed.

I used to believe being wild meant being reckless. Now I know wildness is about freedom.

Freedom to speak. Freedom to feel. Freedom to take up space in a world that once told me I was too much.

Sometimes, I still hear the echoes of those old voices, be quiet, don't make a fuss, you're too emotional. But now I smile. Because they no longer hold power. Those words belong to a time when I didn't know my worth.

Now I know better.

My wild woman doesn't roar all the time. She doesn't need to. She lives in the calm certainty that I am enough, exactly as I am.

She whispers to me when I'm tempted to shrink: Stand tall, love. Speak anyway. She reminds me that being kind doesn't mean being silent. That softness and strength can coexist. That boundaries are a form of love, for others, and for myself.

I rise every day with her beside me, guiding me toward authenticity. She is the spark in my laughter, the steel in my spine, the grace in my "no."

The world hasn't changed. People still criticize, judge, and misunderstand. But I have changed, and that has made all the difference.

I walk through life now with my head high, not because I have all the answers, but because I finally know the question that matters:

What would my wild woman do? She would live boldly. She would love deeply. She would never apologize for shining. And so I do.

I was once silenced, now sovereign. Once hidden, now free. Once too much, now more than enough.

My wild woman didn't rise to make me someone new. She rose to help me remember who I've been all along.

"Wild woman are an unexplainable spark of life. They ooze freedom and seek awareness, they belong to nobody but themselves yet give a piece of who they are to everyone they meet."
~Nikki Rowe~

PART 2

WOMEN LIKE ME

"Women who believe in each other create armies that will win
kingdoms and wars."
~Nikita Gill~

THE WOMEN LIKE ME COMMUNITY
A PLACE TO BELONG, A SPACE TO WRITE, A MOVEMENT TO INSPIRE

If you're not already part of the Women Like Me Community, I invite you to step into a space where women come together to uplift, empower, and share their voices. This is more than just a social network, it's a writing community filled with women who have stories to tell, wisdom to share, and dreams to bring to life.

Here, you'll find connection, encouragement, and inspiration from like-minded women who understand the journey of life, the power of words, and the importance of lifting each other up.

Whether you're a seasoned writer, a first-time author, or someone who simply wants to share your truth, this is a place where your words matter.

Throughout the year, we collaborate on Women Like Me Community books, like the one you are reading now. Every woman in our community is invited to contribute, and there's no cost to participate, just a willingness to share your story and inspire others.

If you've ever dreamed of becoming a published author, this is your chance to take that first step in a supportive and welcoming environment.

More than just a writing group, the Women Like Me Community is a movement. Whether you're a working professional, an entrepreneur, or a stay-at-home mom, you'll find mentors, role models, and friendships that will help you grow, not just as a writer, but as a woman embracing her full potential.

If you've been searching for a place where you can be seen, heard, and valued, this is it.

Your story matters. Your voice matters. You matter.

Don't wait, join us today and start writing the next chapter of your life!

Our group is located on Facebook...

Write Like a Woman – Empowered by Women Like Me

https://www.facebook.com/groups/879482909307802

"I really think a champion is defined not by their wins but by how they can recover when they fall."
~Serena Williams~

THE BOOK SERIES

Everyone has a story. And oftentimes, those stories can be powerful things that help us learn and grow.

But for some people, their stories can be a source of pain. They may feel like they can't escape their past or that their story is holding them back from living their best lives.

If you're one of those people, know that you're not alone. And more importantly, know that there is hope. There are ways to turn your personal story into something positive and to find healing from the past.

One way is to share your story with others. This can be incredibly cathartic, and it can also help others who have been through similar experiences. You process your feelings and work through any trauma you may be carrying around.

And finally, don't forget that your story doesn't define you.

- You are more than your history.
- You are more than your pain.

- You are more than your mistakes.
- You are more than your story.
- You are strong, you are brave, and you are enough.

So don't let your story hold you back.

Writing about your past can be very beneficial, both emotionally and psychologically. You can increase your feelings of well-being and even improve your physical health. When you write about your past experiences, you relive them in your mind. This can help you to process difficult or traumatic events, and it can also provide you with some closure.

Additionally, writing about your past can help you better understand yourself and work through any unresolved issues. It can also allow you to see yourself in a new light, which can be both healing and empowering.

In addition to helping, you emotionally, writing about your past can also be beneficial physically.

Studies have shown that expressive writing can help to reduce stress, anxiety, and depression. It can also help to improve your immune system function and promote a sense of calm. So, if you're feeling stressed or overwhelmed, consider picking up a pen and starting to write.

We only have one shot at this life, and it's our only shot. There are no do-overs. There are no second chances. So, we better make the most of it.

We only have this moment right here, right now, and it's the only moment that matters.

We are only given so much time on this planet and must spend it wisely.

We only have so much energy and want to spend it on things that bring us joy.

We only have so much love and want to give it to people who appreciate it.

If you're a woman with life experiences, the world wants to hear from you. Visit my website at www.juliefairhurst.com and get in touch. The world will be waiting.

A story is powerful. It can draw you in, take you on a journey, and leave you lasting impressions. That's why I love listening to other people's stories.

Everyone has a story, and I'm always eager to hear a new one.

I want to hear from you. You can reach me by visiting my website and letting me know you're ready to tell your story. The world is waiting to hear what you have to say.

Get in touch today!

Women Like Me Stories www.juliefairhurst.com there you'll find the Author Form to fill out and get started!

"I am not afraid... I was born to do this."
~Joan of Arc~

MORE FROM WOMEN LIKE ME

Books are available on Amazon or the Women Like Me Stories website www.wlmbookstore.com. If you can't find the book you are looking for, contact me, and I can help.

Or if you would like an autographed copy, please email at julie@ changeyourpath.ca

Women Like Me Book Series

This is a collection in which women open their hearts, sharing chapters of their lives to inspire and guide others on their journey through life.

- Women Like Me – A Celebration of Courage and Triumphs
- Women Like Me – Stories of Resilience and Courage
- Women Like Me – A Tribute to the Brave and Wise
- Women Like Me – Breaking Through the Silence
- Women Like Me – From Loss to Living
- Women Like Me – Healing and Acceptance
- Women Like Me – Reclaiming Our Power
- Women Like Me – Whispers of Warriors: Women Who Refused to Stay Broken
- Women Like Me – Embracing the Unseen – The Courage to Surrender
- Women Like Me - Transforming Pain Into Wisdom and Love
- Women Like Me - When Life Breaks You Open - Moments That Change Everything
- Women Like Me – Beautiful, Broken, Becoming: Real Stories GrowingThrough Chaos, Self-Doubt, And Second Chances

Women Like Me Community Book Series

The community books are a testament to the power of our beautiful members from all around the world. These remarkable women share their thoughts, experiences, and wisdom, creating books of inspiration and guidance for all.

- Women Like Me Community – Messages to My Younger Self
- Women Like Me Community – Sharing Words of Gratitude
- Women Like Me Community – Sharing What We Know to Be True
- Women Like Me Community – Journal for Self-Discovery
- Women Like Me Community – Sharing Life's Important Lessons
- Women Like Me Community – Having Better Relationships
- Women Like Me Community – Honoring the Women in Our Lives
- Women Like Me Community – Letters to Our Future Selves
- Women Like Me Community – The Warrior Within
- Women Like Me Community – Whisper's Within the Power of Women's Intuition
- Women Like Me Community – Dreams That Speak the Power Of Women's Dreams
- Women Like Me Community – Graceful Guidance Treasured Advice and Love From One Generation to The Next
- Women Like Me Community – Whispers of the Heart True Stories of Love and Wisdom
- Women Like Me Community – Lessons From Mom
- Women Like Me Community - The Quiet Ones Who Saved Us: Pets That Became Our Lifeline
- Women Like Me Community – Wild Woman Rising: The Sacred, Untamed, and Unapologetic Truths of Womanhood

Women Like Me in Kenya

100% of the profits go directly to these 26 Kenyan Authors. The Women Like Me Program covers all costs of producing and publishing Kenyan books.

These women are mostly widowed and live in extreme poverty. They use the proceeds to pay school fees so their children can get an education. No school fees mean children cannot go to school. They also purchase food and clothing for their children.

If you would like to support these amazing women in Kenya, please reach out to Julie at julie@changeyourpath.ca

- Women Like Me – Strong Women in Kenya
- Women Like Me – Through the Eyes of Kenyan Women
- Women Like Me – The Children of Kenya
- Women Like Me – Kenyan Women Share Their Strength, Wisdom and Love

SALES AND PERSONAL GROWTH

Julie Fairhurst offers a wealth of knowledge through her books on achieving success in business and life. With a remarkable 34-year career as an entrepreneur, her expertise spans sales, marketing, promotion, and writing.

At her website you'll find resources, authors, digital course and more.

www.juliefairhurst.com

- The Julie Fairhurst Story – Healing Generations, One Story at a Time
- From Idea to Bestseller – Writing for Self-Help Authors
- Positivity Makes All the Difference
- Powerful Persuasion – Unlocking the Five Key Strategies for Business Success
- Transferring Enthusiasm - The Sales Book for Your Business Growth
- Agent Matchmaker: How to Find Your Real Estate Soulmate"
- Agent Etiquette – 14 Things You Didn't Learn in Real Estate School
- 7 Keys to Success – How to Become a Real Estate Badass
- 30 Days to Real Estate Action – Real Strategies & Real Connections
- Why Agents Quit the Business

"I am a strong woman, with or without this other person, with or
without this job,
and with or without these tight pants."
~Queen Latifah~

JULIE FAIRHURST
EMPOWERING WOMEN THROUGH STORYTELLING AND INFLUENCE

Julie Fairhurst is the visionary **Founder of the Women Like Me Book Program**, a groundbreaking initiative that has empowered over **180 women to become published authors**. With **300+ true-life stories published** and **over 30 books released**, many of which have achieved **#1 Best Seller status**, Julie has created a platform where women can share their voices, inspire others, and leave a lasting legacy.

What sets the **Women Like Me Book Program** apart is its commitment to accessibility and empowerment. Some women in the program are given the opportunity to **become published authors at no cost**, ensuring that every woman, regardless of financial circumstances, has the chance to share her truth with the world.

Beyond publishing, Julie is a **renowned speaker, trainer, and educator** with **34 years of expertise in sales and marketing**. A **Master Persuader** with deep insights into human behavior, she specializes in helping **women entrepreneurs** build **influence, establish authority, and increase revenue** through powerful storytelling, strategic marketing, and high-impact sales techniques.

Julie's personal journey, marked by **overcoming adversity, loss, and hardship**, has fueled her passion for **mentoring women**, guiding them to **rise above their challenges, own their stories, and embrace their fullest potential**.

Whether through her books, coaching, or speaking engagements, Julie's mission is clear: **to inspire, uplift, and transform lives —one story at a time.**

Connect with Julie...

- Social Media – Julie Fairhurst Women Like Me
- Website – www.juliefairhurst.com
- Email: julie@changeyourpath.ca
- Media Kit – www.juliefairhurst.com

"It's okay to be scared. Being scared means you're about to do something really, really brave."
~Mandy Hale~

www.ingramcontent.com/pod-product-compliance
Lightning Source LLC
Chambersburg PA
CBHW060805050426
42449CB00008B/1539